ROCKETRY

A FIRST BOOK

ROCKETRY

FROM GODDARD
TO SPACE TRAVEL
BY CHRISTOPHER
LAMPTON

FRANKLIN WATTS
NEW YORK • LONDON • TORONTO
SYDNEY • 1988

Photographs courtesy of:
The Bettmann Archive, Inc.: pp. 13 , 18, 50;
Sovfoto: pp. 24, 42, 52, 60;
NASA: pp. 29, 30, 48, 59, 65, 73, 77, 83;
UPI/Bettmann Archive: pp. 36, 37;
U.S. Army Photograph: p. 46; Photri: p. 70.
Illustrations by Vantage Art

Library of Congress Cataloging-in-Publication Data

Lampton, Christopher.
Rocketry: from Goddard to space travel.

Bibliography: p.
Includes index.
Summary: Presents the history of rocketry from
the "Chinese arrow" to the space shuttle with emphasis
on the work of such people as Congreve, Tsiolkovsky,
Goddard, and Von Braun.
1. Rocketry—Juvenile literature. [1. Rocketry]
I. Title.
TL782.5.L28   1988   621.43′56′09   87-21558
ISBN 0-531-10483-4

CONTENTS

ROCKETRY

INTRODUCTION

Next time you see a rocket shoot into the sky in a Fourth of July fireworks display, you might remember that such fireworks have been around for at least a thousand years.

But these Fourth of July rockets are mere toys, the distant relatives of other, more powerful rockets. It is these more powerful rockets that this book is about.

These rockets have two histories, a history of war and a history of peace.

The first is the history of the missile, beginning hundreds of years ago in China. Today, the distant descendants of the first Chinese missiles are buried deep in underground silos on both sides of the world, waiting to be fired at the push of a button.

The second of these histories began at the turn of the century, in the mind of a brilliant Russian dreamer who believed that rockets were a means of transportation that could someday take human beings to the moon.

In this book, we'll talk mostly about the rocket as a marvelous means of transportation. But it is impossible to escape the history of the rocket as a weapon of war. Ironically, if it weren't for war, we would never have gone to the moon.

As you will see.

CHAPTER

1

DAWN OF
THE ROCKET

The British soldiers, newly arrived in a strange foreign land, knew that they were in for a fight, but they had never expected the enemy to be armed with weapons that flew through the sky trailing fire behind them. It wasn't the first time that the soldiers had seen rockets—fireworks were a common sight at holiday celebrations—but they had never seen rockets used as weapons of war. The rockets had never been aimed at them!

The occasion was the first battle of Seringapatam, India, in 1792. The British were fighting the rebellious Haidar Ali of Mysore. If the British thought they could easily win the battle, they were badly mistaken. The Indians had organized a portion of their troops into rocket brigades. According to some accounts, the rockets that they fired were noisier than they were dangerous. But other eyewitnesses described sharpened bamboo poles attached to some of the rockets, which rained down on the British soldiers like deadly spears. Each rocket could travel about 1,000 yards (914 m), not quite a quarter of a mile. That's not far by modern standards, but far enough to penetrate deep into the British forces. In 1799, when the British again went to war at Seringapatam, they once again were met by a volley of rockets, just as terrifying as the first.

Those battles changed history, because when the British troops returned home, they brought word (and a few rockets) to Colonel William Congreve (1772–1828) of the Royal Laboratory of Woolwich Arsenal in London. And it was Congreve who turned the manufacture of rockets into a military science.

Nobody knows when rockets were invented, or when they were first used. Almost certainly they were first used somewhere in China, because that's where the earliest historical records of rockets have been found, from many hundreds of years ago. Battles involving rockets took place as early as the twelfth century, and possibly much earlier.

But rocketlike devices existed even earlier than that. Hero of Alexandria (Egypt), in the first century A.D., built a small sphere with curved pipes sticking out of it that spun around under its own power. This spinning was caused by powerful jets of steam rushing out of the pipes, which forced the sphere to spin on its pedestal. The steam was created by heating water inside the sphere.

This is similar to the way in which rockets are propelled, but actual rockets weren't built until another invention made them possible—black powder, which we know today as gunpowder.

Black powder is made by mixing sulphur, saltpeter, and charcoal. It was invented by the Chinese sometime around the tenth century, and was used to make firecrackers, which the Chinese called *Pao Chang*.

It's hard to say just when black powder was first used to build rockets, and not all modern histories of the subject agree. According to historian David Baker, an early Chinese history book—the *Complete Compendium of Military Classics*—provides evidence that rockets had been built and were ready for use in battle shortly after the year 1000. They may have been used even earlier in fireworks displays, which to this day remain a popular use for small rockets. The Chinese war rockets came to be known as "fire arrows" and were used to repel invaders, such as the Mongols. How far these not fired through the air as rapidly as the bullets that they have just discharged?

The answer is that the pitcher is bigger than the baseball, just as soldiers are bigger than bullets. The force of the recoil—the backwards push—is just as strong as the forward push imparted to ball or bullet, but a large object such as a human being can absorb that force with less movement. Further, a person with both feet braced against solid ground is in turn imparting a lot of that force to Earth itself, which can absorb it without noticeable movement.

When gunpowder inside a rocket tube is set on fire, tiny particles of gas called *atoms* are pushed out of the open end of the tube. (The other end of the tube must be closed.) Just as a baseball pushes its pitcher according to Newton's third law, these speeding atoms push the gunpowder, and the rocket tube surrounding it, in the opposite direction. If the open end of the rocket tube is pointing straight down, the rocket will be pushed straight up.

Of course, the atoms of gas are very, very small compared to the body of the rocket. How can these tiny atoms push a rocket into the air? Well, the atoms are moving at extremely high speeds. Even though each atom gives the rocket only a small push, there are billions and billions of atoms in the gas and all those tiny pushes add up. In fact, it is possible for the rocket, pushed by all of those speeding atoms, to achieve speeds greater than that of the atoms themselves.

ANOTHER WAY TO
LOOK AT IT

If you find Newton's third law a little hard to grasp, you might want to look at rockets in a slightly different manner. Imagine that you have a large metal box, inside of which is a gas. Any kind of gas— air, for instance—will do. The box is tightly sealed so that the gas cannot escape.

Through some magic arrangement, you now heat the gas inside

the box. This gas, as we saw, is made up of atoms. (Actually, it is made up of tiny chains of atoms called *molecules*, but we won't worry about that here.) As the gas gets hotter, these atoms begin to move around very quickly, battering themselves against the inside of the box.

Question: As the atoms bang against the inner wall of the box with greater and greater violence, will the box move?

Answer: No. The box will not move. Why? Because the atoms within the box are moving randomly, in all directions. There are billions and billions of these atoms, and every time a few million atoms are flung against one wall of the box by the heat, another few million are thrown at the opposite wall. These atoms *do* push against the walls, but they cancel one another out by pushing in all directions at the same time. The box cannot move in any one direction, so it moves in no direction at all.

But now suppose that we remove one wall from the box. The atoms that are pushed in that direction by the heat will have no wall to push against; they will simply escape into the surrounding air. The atoms pushing against the opposite wall will no longer have their movement canceled out, and the box will actually move—away from the missing wall!

This pretty much describes a rocket: a box, or chamber, in which one wall has been removed, with a hot gas inside. The gas pushing in the opposite direction from the open end of the rocket pushes the rocket forward, because it is not canceled out by gas pushing the other way. The rocket will move away from the hole at the end of the chamber, though the exact direction in which the rocket moves can be controlled in other ways. This also describes the twirling sphere of Hero of Alexandria, which used hot steam as the gas that propelled it—except that Hero's device could only move in circles!

THE ROCKET'S RED GLARE

The modern age of war rockets began when the Englishman William Congreve was asked to produce a rocket modeled on those returned from the battle of Seringapatam. Congreve, in fact, wrote an entire book entitled *A Concise Account on the Origin and Progress of the Rocket System*, published in 1804, in which he discussed his theories of rocketry, especially their use as weapons. According to Congreve, the chief advantage of rockets as weapons was that, unlike cannons and other guns, they didn't produce any recoil. (Actually, as we saw earlier, it is recoil that causes the rocket to fly. But this recoil is contained entirely in the rocket and its fuel. It doesn't affect anything, or anyone, in the vicinity of the rocket—unless they are foolish enough to stand in the flow of hot gas that propels the rocket into the air.) This meant that rockets could be used in places where cannons could not, such as on board ships. (Cannons have been used on board ships, but only with great caution. The recoil can cause the ships to rock violently in the water, and even to overturn.)

Congreve built several different types of rockets, some of which could fly as far as 3,000 yards (2,743 m). These rockets were iron tubes with cone-shaped heads, and a rod, called a guiding stick, attached to one side to keep them from wobbling in flight. The largest were about 3.5 feet (108 cm) in length and weighed 32 pounds (14.5 kg).

The British army wasted no time in bringing these rockets into battle. In November of 1805, ten boats loaded with "Congreve rockets" were sent to do battle with the French at the city of Boulogne, France, but the rocketeers were repelled by a violent storm which sank several of the ships. The next year, however, Congreve rockets were fired at Copenhagen, with highly destructive results.

Over the next few decades, the British used rockets in many battles, including one famous battle against the United States during the War of 1812. During the battle, at Baltimore's Fort McHenry, a young poet named Francis Scott Key watched the rocket bombardment and wrote a poem about "the rocket's red glare/the bombs bursting in air." Later, set to music, that poem became the American national anthem, *The Star-Spangled Banner*.

By the middle of the nineteenth century, however, the rocket

A British rocket troop in 1814

lost favor as a weapon of war. It was replaced by other, more conventional, weapons, which had become as powerful as rockets and were much easier (and less dangerous) to use. As a weapon, the rocket was forgotten for nearly a century, but in the meantime a new use for the rocket would be found:

Rockets could take human beings to the moon—and beyond!

CHAPTER

2

CONQUERORS OF THE VOID

The planet Earth is actually a very small place. Although it is large enough to hold several billion people, it is only the tiniest part of the universe around it.

To put things into perspective, consider that Earth is about 8,000 miles (12,880 km) in diameter (the distance through Earth at the longest point) and about 25,000 miles (40,250 km) in circumference (the distance around Earth's equator). This means that there is no point on Earth's surface that is more than 12,500 miles (20,125 km) away from you (or 8,000 miles, if you measure through the center of the planet). By contrast, the moon is more than 240,000 miles (386,400 km) away from you—and the moon is Earth's nearest neighbor! The planet Venus, at its closest, is about 26 *million* miles (42 million km) from Earth—and Venus is the closest planet to Earth! The sun, which shines so brightly in the daytime sky that we cannot look directly at it without harming our eyes, is 93 million miles (153.6 million km) away!

Even the sun is just a hop, skip, and jump away compared to the stars, the nearest of which is trillions of miles distant. Through large telescopes, astronomers can see other objects so far away that the light from them takes billions of years to reach us—and light travels at a speed of 186,282 miles (300,000 km) per *second*!

A person who travels 10,000 miles (16,000 km) across the surface of this planet can be considered well traveled—on Earth. But a journey that would take you nearly halfway around the world would barely take you any distance at all through the universe as a whole. Our planet is almost totally explored, but an unimaginably large universe lies beyond this planet that human beings have barely visited.

Is it possible for human beings to travel through the universe beyond Earth? Yes, but it certainly isn't easy. Our planet is covered with a thin shell of air known as the atmosphere, and it is only in the last half of the twentieth century that we have learned how to travel outside of this shell. Beyond the atmosphere lies *outer space*, and the key to traveling in outer space is the rocket.

THE UNIVERSE BEYOND

Until a few centuries ago, no one was aware that there was a universe beyond Earth to travel in. The ancient Greeks thought that the heavens were a series of glassy spheres, with the stars and planets embedded in them—not the kind of place one would explore at length, though it might be interesting to visit. This belief endured until the seventeenth century, when astronomers like Galileo began to turn powerful optical instruments called telescopes on the skies . . . and realized that the lights in the night sky were suns and planets in their own right.

Once again, it was the great Isaac Newton who unlocked the secrets of the universe beyond Earth's atmosphere. He showed that the Earth and the other planets, such as Mercury, Venus, Mars, Jupiter, and Saturn, moved around the sun in great circles (ellipses, actually) called orbits. The moon, in turn, moved in an orbit around Earth.

The planets in this *solar* (sun) *system* are each a world in its own right, many of them larger than Earth. The moon, though it however, the fuel could be stored in one chamber, then pumped into another chamber, where it would be burned. By controlling this flow, the rocket could be speeded up, slowed down, or brought to a complete stop and then started again.

— Encyclopedia info on How a Rocket Moves

MULTISTAGE ROCKETRY

Another important idea introduced by Tsiolkovsky (although it had been used in the making of fireworks for hundreds of years) was the multistage rocket. A multistage rocket is a large rocket made of several smaller rockets, stacked one on top of another. What is the advantage of this? Well, in order to reach high speeds and travel long distances, a rocket must carry large amounts of fuel. But to carry all of that fuel, the rocket must be very large, and very heavy.

This creates a paradox. A small rocket can fly at high speeds, because it is very light. But it cannot travel far, because it cannot carry enough fuel. A large rocket can carry a large amount of fuel, but it cannot travel fast because it is so heavy.

Fortunately, a rocket becomes lighter as it flies, because it is constantly ejecting atoms of fuel. Thus a large rocket may be very heavy when it takes off, and may move at a relatively slow speed. But as it burns up its fuel it becomes lighter and lighter, and can fly faster and faster. Unfortunately, the rocket itself will not grow smaller. A large rocket, built to hold millions of gallons of fuel, will still be a large rocket when most of the fuel inside it is burned up.

A multistage rocket, on the other hand, can actually grow smaller as it burns its fuel. Suppose, for instance, that we have a rocket with three stages. Each stage is a complete rocket, and the three stages are stacked on top of one another. When we launch the rocket, the first stage—the one on the bottom—begins burning its fuel and producing thrust. Slowly (because it is large and heavy) the rocket lifts into the air.

As soon as the first stage has burned all of its fuel, it is dropped back to Earth. (Today, multistage rockets are launched over the ocean, so that the stages won't fall on top of unlucky bystanders.) Now we turn on the second stage, which has already been delivered to a high altitude by the first stage. With the first stage gone, the rocket is lighter and doesn't need as much fuel to reach high speeds. When the second stage runs out of fuel, it, too, is dropped, and the rocket becomes lighter still.

Tsiolkovsky remained interested in rockets for the rest of his life. He believed that the future of humankind lay in outer space. According to Tsiolkovsky, "Earth is the cradle of mankind; but one cannot remain forever in the cradle." He envisioned a time when people could live in giant space stations that orbit Earth like artificial moons.

A FORCE CALLED GRAVITY

How could we create an artificial moon? Once again, this was an idea conceived centuries before Tsiolkovsky by Isaac Newton, who was responsible for so many of the basic ideas that in time became part of rocketry. Newton showed that moons go around planets, and planets go around the sun, because of gravity and momentum. Gravity is a force produced by all objects in the universe, a force that attracts other objects. Large objects, like stars—our sun, for instance—produce enough gravity to attract planets. Planets produce enough gravity to attract moons. Human beings are not large enough to produce any noticeable gravity, though we do produce a small amount. However, the powerful gravity of the planet Earth attracts us toward the ground, which is why we cannot simply leap into space anytime we feel like it.

Momentum is the tendency of an object in motion to remain in motion. (This is Newton's First Law of Motion.) When a moving object—an object with momentum—is attracted by the gravity of another, very large object, its movement is bent by gravity. If it is moving at the proper angle to the large object, it can go into orbit around it.

Newton demonstrated this with an imaginary experiment. Suppose that you have a superpowerful cannon on top of a mountain. When you fire the cannon, the cannonball tries to move in a straight line out of the mouth of the cannon (because of its momentum), but it will also be attracted toward the ground by Earth's gravity. Therefore it will fall to the ground in a long curve, moving sideways and downward at the same time. Now suppose you trade your cannon for a more powerful cannon and fire the cannonball at a faster speed. The cannonball will travel farther before it hits the ground. If you fire your cannonball at an extremely fast speed, it will actually fall around the curve of Earth, and never hit the ground. It will continue to "fall" around Earth forever, chasing the ground but never hitting it. It will go into orbit.

Of course, we cannot perform this experiment in the real world, because there is no cannon powerful enough to put a cannonball into orbit and because friction with the air would quickly bring the cannonball to a halt. But suppose we used a rocket (which would be much more powerful than any cannon) and fired the cannonball *above* Earth's atmosphere, so there would be no air friction. We could then put the cannonball into orbit. It would become an artificial moon, or *satellite*, of Earth.

Tsiolkovsky knew that a rocket would have to move quite rapidly to put an artificial satellite into orbit: at least 5 miles (8 km) per second. This speed is called *orbital velocity*. To escape from the gravity of Earth altogether, a rocket would need to fly even faster: 7 miles (11.3 km) per second. This speed is called *escape velocity*.

Tsiolkovsky's work was largely ignored for most of his life. In his later years, though, he became something of a Russian hero. After his death, his house was made into a museum.

GODDARD'S DREAM HISTORY OF THE ROCKET

Tsiolkovsky was the father of modern rocket theory. He understood how rockets worked, and what they could do, but he never tried to build one. At about the same time as Tsiolkovsky was writing books in Russia about his ideas, another great scientist in the United

Go to space vehicles book

States was turning rocket theory into reality. His name was Robert Hutchings Goddard (1882–1945).

Goddard was a professor of physics at Clark University in Massachusetts. Like Tsiolkovsky, he was fascinated by rockets and space travel. As a child, he had read science fiction novels by Jules Verne and H. G. Wells and dreamed of traveling to the moon and beyond. He began building rockets in 1915, some of which flew as high as 500 feet (152 m) in the air. When the United States entered World War I, Goddard experimented with rockets for the Army. After the war, he received money from the Smithsonian Institution to further his research. In 1919, he wrote a paper entitled *A Method of Reaching Extreme Altitudes*, which the Smithsonian published.

In Goddard's time, most people considered space travel to be a silly fantasy, and Goddard knew that he had better keep his ideas about sending human beings to the moon to himself. When he wrote the paper for the Smithsonian, he spoke mainly of using rockets to launch scientific instruments to study the upper atmosphere. But in the final section he mentioned the possibility of sending a rocket to the moon, where it could splash bright red flash powder across the surface to show astronomers that it had arrived.

It was this suggestion that made Goddard famous, at least briefly. In newspapers around the country Goddard was laughed at as the "moon man," who wanted to spend government money to go to the moon. *The New York Times* published an editorial entitled "A Severe Strain on Credulity," in which it stated that Goddard "seems to lack the knowledge ladled out daily in high schools" because he failed to understand that rockets could not move in outer space. Apparently, the unnamed editorialist believed that rockets flew because their thrust pushed against the air; in fact, it was the *New York Times* that showed its fundamental ignorance of science, since Newton had shown nearly three hundred years earlier that this was not so. The *Times* finally retracted this editorial in 1969, on the day that Neil Armstrong and Edwin Aldrin became the first human beings to land on the moon.

This sort of reaction may explain why Goddard avoided publicity throughout his career. He preferred to work alone, without outside interference.

In the early part of his career, Goddard was not familiar with the work of Tsiolkovsky, probably because the Russian scientist was virtually unknown outside of his native country. Nonetheless, Goddard came to the same conclusion in his work that Tsiolkovsky had, that the future of rocketry was in liquid fuels. But unlike the Russian, Goddard actually built liquid-fuel rockets!

By the mid-1930s, Goddard's rockets were flying at speeds of more than 500 miles (805 km) per hour, soaring a mile and a half into the air. Goddard patented hundreds of devices related to rockets, including sophisticated nozzles for releasing the hot gases that propelled the rocket and elaborate systems of pipes and chambers for transporting fuel from one part of the rocket to another. (See Goddard's 1937 drawing on the facing page, showing pressure line, gasoline line, liquid oxygen line, supports between tanks, and wiring diagram. Many years later, when the United States was preparing to launch astronauts into orbit around Earth, the United States government paid Goddard's estate one million dollars for the use of his patents.)

In his lifetime, Goddard attracted relatively little attention from the United States government. In part, this may have been because Goddard was a quiet, private person. But there is little question that Goddard's true importance to modern science was not recognized until long after his death in 1945.

Apparently the United States had little time for such ideas as rockets and space travel in the first half of the twentieth century. This oversight allowed the development of rocketry to take place in other countries, in a way that the United States would eventually come to regret.

THE SPACE AGE BEGINS

In Germany, during the 1920s and 1930s, building rockets was something of a fad. And the man who started the fad was Hermann Oberth (1894–). In 1923, Oberth published a book entitled *The Rocket into Interplanetary Space*. Although Oberth's book covered much of the same ground as Goddard's *A Method of Reaching Extreme Altitudes*, he was less shy about discussing the use of rockets for space travel. Like other early rocket pioneers, Oberth believed that the destiny of the human race was in outer space, and that the rocket was the way to get there. In his book, he spelled out the technical details of how rocket travel would be accomplished. Unfortunately, his book was so technical that the average person couldn't understand what he was saying.

This didn't stop his ideas from spreading. By 1929, German interest in rocketry was strong enough that Oberth was invited to become a member of a newly founded society called *Verein fur Raumschiffahrt*—the Society for Space Travel, or VfR for short.

THE SOCIETY FOR SPACE TRAVEL

The VfR brought together an extraordinary group of people interested in amateur rocketry, including Wernher von Braun (1912–

1977), who would later become a major figure in the American space program, and Willy Ley (1906–1969), who went on to publish several important histories of rocketry.

The group found an abandoned munitions dump near Berlin, where they could perform their experiments. They called it their *raketenflugplatz*, or "place for flying rockets." There, they built several small demonstration rockets, some of which flew as high as a mile. But within a few years of the founding of the VfR, German politics began to change. The National Socialist Party, better known as the Nazis, came to power. The leader of the Nazis was Adolph Hitler, who was intent on conquering the world. The members of the VfR feared that the German secret police, called the Gestapo, would interfere with their work. To protect themselves from this kind of interference, they turned to the German army, which they knew would be interested in rockets.

The Army was indeed interested. A decade and a half earlier, the Germans had been defeated in World War I. The Treaty of Versailles, signed by the major world leaders at the end of the war, forbade the Germans from developing most types of weapons. However, the treaty said nothing about the development of rockets. A group of military rocket experts turned out in 1932 to watch the young rocketeers of the VfR launch a rocket that they called *Mirak*, short for "minimum rocket." The demonstration went poorly, but the experts were impressed with the young rocketeers themselves and asked for more demonstrations. One of these military experts, Captain Walter Dornberger, would be chief of German rocket development from 1931 to 1945.

Later that year, the Army Weapons Department asked Wernher von Braun to work for them as a civilian rocket researcher. According to those who knew him, von Braun was a charming young man with a boundless enthusiasm for rockets, so much enthusiasm that it was difficult for those around him not to share it. Like Tsiolkovsky and Goddard and Oberth, he dreamed of a time when human beings would fly to the moon. But he knew that the only way he would ever be given the money he needed to build powerful rockets would be to work for the army, which was more interested in using the rockets to carry bombs than for space flight. Along with other former members of the VfR, von Braun went to work for the Army Weapons Department in 1932, building liquid-fuel rockets under the command of Captain Dornberger.

ROCKETS FOR WAR

The German Army needed a secret testing ground for new rockets, and so Dornberger and von Braun went in search of one. They found it on the coast of the Baltic Sea, near the village of Peenemunde, at the mouth of the Peene River. There they built a large facility for building, testing, and thinking about rockets.

Von Braun's first major project with the Army was the Aggregate-1 rocket, better known as the A-1. It was a small test rocket, and not very impressive in its capabilities, but other more powerful rockets followed. The most impressive of these was the A-4, which von Braun's team of now highly experienced rocket engineers began building in the late 1930s.

But by that time, Adolph Hitler had begun his planned conquest of Europe, and World War II was under way. The A-4 was renamed the *Vergeltungswaffen Zwei* ("Vengeance Weapon Two"), but it quickly became known by the abbreviation V-2.

When it was finally completed in 1944, the V-2 was the most powerful rocket the world had ever known, the first true missile. It had a range of hundreds of miles. A launching site for the V-2s was built on the Dutch coast, which was by then occupied by the Nazis. The missiles were fired at France and Belgium, but mostly at England, where more than two thousand people were killed by these terrifying flying bombs that rained down out of the sky.

The modern age of missile warfare had begun.

But within a year, the terror of the V-2 bombings was over. Nazi Germany fell before the combined onslaught of its enemies, which included the United States and the Soviet Union. As the Allied troops swept across a defeated Germany, von Braun and his Peenemunde

Above: in the closing days of World War II, U.S. army troops captured this railroad train stocked with V-2 missiles, apparently being transported to a launch site. Opposite: this is an actual launching of a German V-2 rocket at Peenemunde, the major Nazi guided missile research-and-testing center.

rocketeers huddled together to contemplate their future. They still wanted to build rockets. They had never really been interested in creating missiles, preferring to think that their rockets would one day take human beings into space. They knew that their knowledge of rocketry would make them welcome guests in either the United States or the Soviet Union. Which country should they go to? They chose the United States.

However, they knew that Soviet troops were drawing closer every day, and that they might find themselves involuntarily taken to the Soviet Union if they did not act quickly. Von Braun's brother was sent, by bicycle, to a nearby village, where he surrendered, in the name of the entire rocket team, to the United States.

Years later, von Braun and his fellow engineers would realize their dream of sending human beings to the moon. But not before another country, which the world had believed to be technologically backward, had made the first great leap into the space age.

A ROCKETEER NAMED KOROLEV

While the young rocketeers of the VfR dreamed of launching rockets into space, scientists in another country not far away were making similar plans, with about as much reason to think that they could succeed.

In the Soviet Union during the 1930s, amateur rocketry was a popular hobby, just as it was in Germany. And, as in Germany, politics got in the way of the rocketeers.

One young Russian rocketeer was named Sergei Korolev (1907–1966). He was a talented designer of rockets and airplanes, and soon found a position designing aircraft for the military, though like von Braun and Goddard and so many other rocketry pioneers, he dreamed of a day when rockets would fly in outer space. Later, he would make these dreams come true, becoming the father of Russian rocketry and the man responsible for the first human beings to orbit Earth. But in the 1930s he was another Russian citizen caught up in the deadly politics of Josef Stalin.

Stalin had become the ruler of the Soviet Union when V. I. Lenin died in 1924. Like Hitler in Germany, Stalin wanted to be an absolute dictator, and so he set out to arrest, deport, and even murder all of his enemies. In the 1930s, thousands of prominent Soviet citizens disappeared, often in the middle of the night, shipped away to distant prison camps, if they were lucky enough not to be put to death on trumped-up charges.

Korolev was one of the unfortunate Russians to incur Stalin's wrath. In 1937 he was arrested and sent away to prison. Fortunately, he had powerful friends who were able to secure him a position designing airplanes while in prison.

At the end of World War II, Stalin's attention turned to rocketry. The dictator was furious that the United States had spirited away the team of German rocket engineers, leaving only a few minor rocket designers to surrender to the Russian army. Korolev, still a prisoner, was given a battery of captured V-2 rockets and told to build more like them.

The Russian engineer was probably delighted to have the chance. The V-2 was the rocket he had dreamed of building in his youth, the key to the exploration of outer space. Of course, the V-2 itself was not powerful enough to penetrate Earth's atmosphere and fly in outer space, but the German engineers had solved many of the problems of building liquid-fuel rockets, and they had given Korolev the key to building rockets that were still more powerful.

In 1953, Stalin died. The politics of the Soviet Union were thrown into confusion as several powerful men fought to become his successor. The winner was a canny Ukrainian peasant named Nikita Khrushchev. When Khrushchev was given a tour of Korolev's rocket factory, he was stunned. He had never imagined that such things existed. He was also impressed by Korolev himself. Years later, Khrushchev wrote in his memoirs: "We had absolute confidence in Comrade Korolev. When he expounded his ideas, you could see passion burning in his eyes, and his reports were always models of clarity. He had unlimited energy and determination, and he was a brilliant organizer."

THE COLD WAR

Korolev was also the solution to a thorny problem that the Soviets faced in the 1950s. During World War II, the United States and the Soviet Union had fought together against Hitler's Germany, but the two countries were not friendly. Many people believed—and still do—that if there were another world war, it would be fought between the United States and the Soviet Union. Throughout the 1950s and early 1960s, a terrible tension existed between these two super-powerful countries. This period of tension came to be known as the Cold War.

At the end of World War II, the United States revealed that it had developed a powerful weapon called the atomic bomb. At war's end, the United States had unleashed this weapon against its foe, the Japanese. (By this time, Germany had already surrendered.)

The Japanese were terrified by this powerful weapon, but so were the Russians. By 1949, they had built an atomic bomb of their own, and by the mid-1950s both the United States and the Soviet Union had built even more powerful weapons called hydrogen bombs.

Just having the bombs wasn't enough. In the event of war, both countries would need a way of dropping the bombs on their enemies. The United States was relying on its large fleet of bomber planes, which could carry the bombs around the world, to any target. The Soviets had no such fleet. They needed another method of sending bombs around the world, and the method they chose was the rocket. Korolev and his team of Soviet rocket engineers were put to work building *intercontinental ballistic missiles*, or *ICBMs* for short. These were rockets, more powerful than any V-2, that could carry heavy atomic bombs over the thousands of miles between the United States and the Soviet Union.

Although Khrushchev knew that he would soon have a powerful fleet of ICBMs, he had a second problem as well. He had to convince the United States that his missiles really worked.

In the 1950s, this was not a simple matter. Most of the world believed that the Soviet Union was technologically backward. When the Soviets bragged of their impressive inventions, other nations laughed, believing that the Soviet inventions were merely sloppy imitations of devices originating in other countries. The Soviets, in large part because of the genius of Korolev, were genuinely ahead of the rest of the world in building rockets, but who would believe them? Khrushchev wasn't going to fire a missile at the United States just to prove that it could be done!

Korolev provided the answer. He suggested to Khrushchev that he be allowed to use one of his new ICBMs to launch an artificial satellite into orbit around Earth. It would be a tremendously valuable scientific achievement. Khrushchev had little interest in scientific achievement, but he knew that the launching of a satellite would impress the United States with the power of Russian missiles. The timing was right. Scientists around the world had declared a period in 1957 and 1958 as the International Geophysical Year, to start studying Earth, and the Soviet satellite would be part of those studies.

By this time, the Soviets had built a rocket-launching base, called the Baikonur Cosmodrome, near the city of Tyuratam. (The Cosmodrome was named after the city of Baikonyr, which was actually several hundred miles away. Apparently this was a ruse intended to mislead spies and saboteurs from other countries.) Korolev returned to Tyuratam under instructions to launch a satellite as quickly as possible. It took him roughly six weeks to prepare for the launch, an amazingly short amount of time. For the *launch vehicle*—the rocket that would lift the satellite into orbit—he chose a rocket known as R-7, which had been intended as an ICBM. Actually, the R-7 would not have made a good ICBM, but it was perfect for launching satellites, which may have been what Korolev had *really* intended.

SPUTNIK

For six weeks, Korolev worked day and night at the launchpad, preparing the R-7 to launch a satellite into space. The satellite,

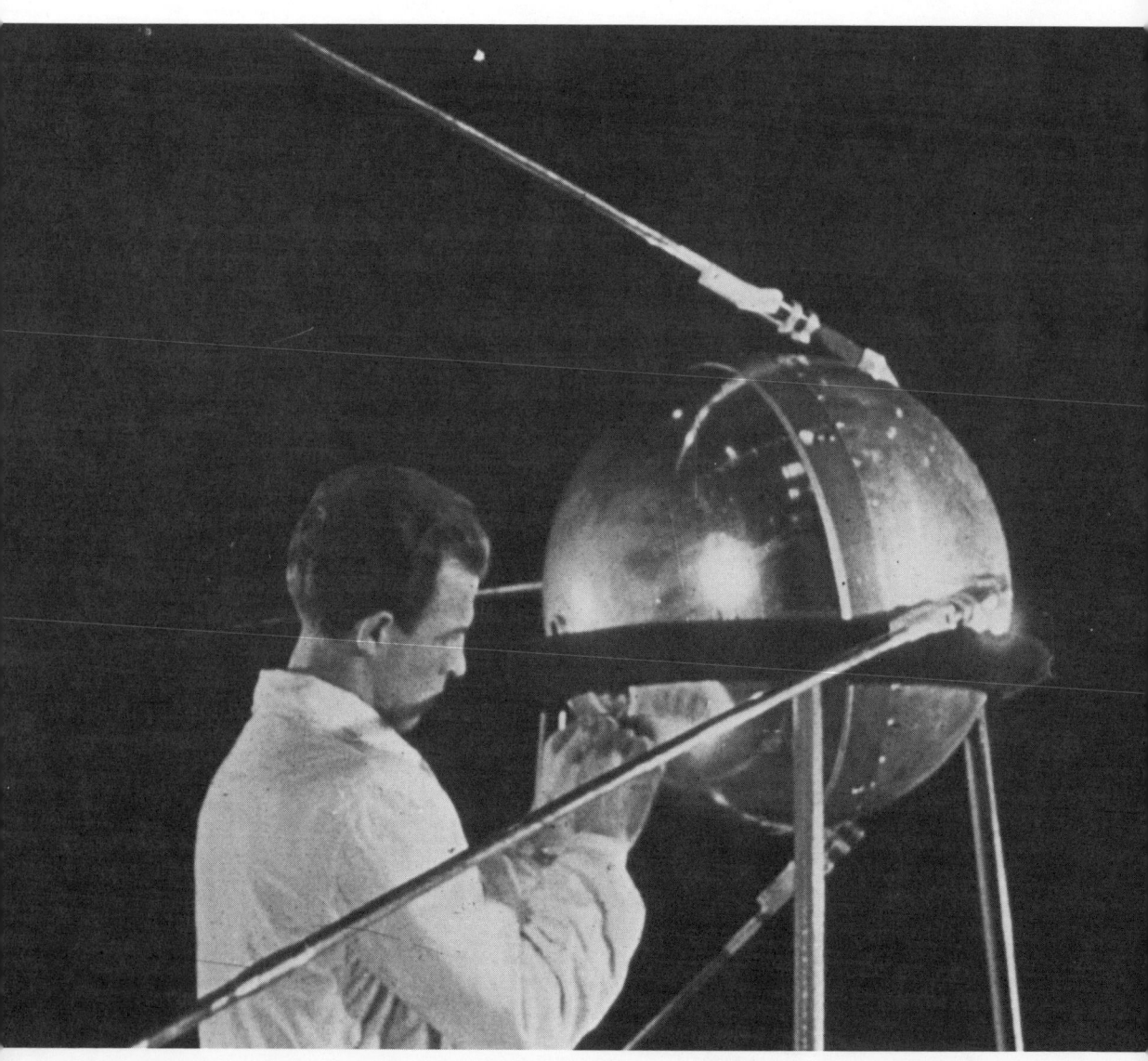

Sputnik 1 *was only 22.8 inches (58 cm)
in diameter and weighed 184.3 pounds (83.6 kg).*

which the Russians called *Sputnik* ("fellow traveler") wasn't very impressive: a metal sphere containing a radio transmitter, a battery pack, and a thermometer. But it was to become the first artificial object to orbit Earth!

Finally, on October 4, 1957—only twenty-nine days after the 100th anniversary of Tsiolkovsky's birth—the rocket was ready. Inside a small bunker 300 feet (91 m) from the pad where the R-7 sat, Korolev gave the order to launch. With a roar, the R-7 rose upward. Four minutes later, it had disappeared into the sky.

The space age had begun. But not even Khrushchev and Korolev could have dreamed what surprises the space age would bring.

CHAPTER

THE GREAT SPACE RACE

After World War II, Wernher von Braun and his rocket engineers came to the United States, where they were expected to do exactly what they had done for Germany: build rockets.

Von Braun went to work for the U.S. Army, launching rockets from the White Sands Air Force Base in the New Mexico desert. His first job was to improve the V-2 rockets that he had brought with him from Germany. One way in which he improved the V-2 was to combine it with a small American rocket called the Wac Corporal, to create a two-stage rocket, like the multistage rockets that Tsiolkovsky had envisioned. The United States V-2 program was code-named Bumper, so the new rocket was christened the Bumper-Wac. By 1949, Bumper-Wac rockets were flying 244 miles (393 km) into the air at speeds of more than 5,000 miles (8,000 km) per hour. Before the Bumper program was over, the launching site was moved from White Sands to a new launching site at Cape Canaveral, Florida, which would later become one of the main centers of the American space program.

MISSILES FOR WAR

In 1950, von Braun and his rocket team, which by now included many American engineers as well as Germans, moved to a new

base at the Redstone Arsenal in Huntsville, Alabama. Once there, they started work on a brand new rocket to be called the Redstone. The Redstone was intended to carry nuclear weapons. However, the range of the Redstone was not very great. At best, it could carry a bomb for 200 miles (322 km), which was not enough to qualify it as a true ICBM.

By the mid-1950s, word reached the United States that the Soviet Union was working on a powerful new fleet of missiles, capable of carrying nuclear weapons for great distances. If this were true—and not everyone believed that it was—it would make the United States bomber fleet obsolete overnight, and place the nation in danger of a sneak nuclear attack from the Soviets.

The Army and the Navy, which had its own missile program, joined together to create a more advanced missile, using the technology already developed for the Redstone. This new missile, called the Jupiter, would be a true ICBM. By May 1957, a Jupiter missile was launched from Cape Canaveral on a 1,600-mile (2,580 km) flight, making it the most powerful United States missile developed up to that time.

Meanwhile, the Air Force had embarked on projects to build two powerful new ICBMs, called the Atlas and the Titan. In addition to the Jupiter, the Navy began work on a smaller missile called the Polaris, which could be launched from submarines deep underwater.

MISSILES FOR PEACE

Von Braun, however, was more interested in exploring space than in building ICBMs. In the midst of all this missile-building, he let it be known that he wanted to launch a satellite. In 1954, he presented

The launching of a Redstone rocket from Cape Canaveral

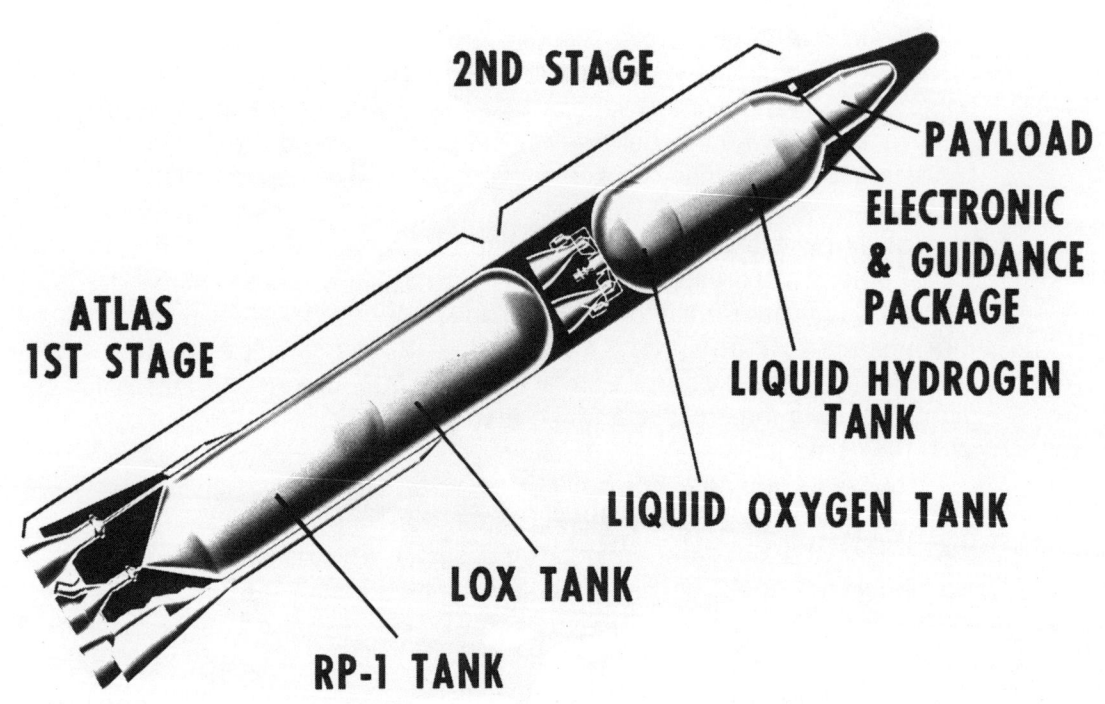

2ND STAGE

PAYLOAD

ELECTRONIC
& GUIDANCE
PACKAGE

ATLAS
1ST STAGE

LIQUID HYDROGEN
TANK

LIQUID OXYGEN TANK

LOX TANK

RP-1 TANK

A two-stage Atlas missile

the Defense Department with a proposal for Project Orbiter, which would use a Jupiter missile to launch a satellite into orbit around Earth.

The Defense Department turned the idea over to the White House, where it was rejected by President Dwight D. Eisenhower. Why did Eisenhower turn down von Braun's proposal? There were several reasons.

As we mentioned in the last chapter, the period from July 1, 1957 to December 31, 1958 had been designated by an international committee as the *International Geophysical Year* (*IGY*). (This "year," you might notice, was actually eighteen months long.) During the IGY, scientists from all over the world would study the planet Earth in great detail. The United States had promised to launch an artifical satellite during this period. The satellite would be filled with scientific instruments to study Earth from high in the sky. The Soviet Union had also promised to launch a satellite, though no one outside of the country actually believed that it would—or could.

President Eisenhower knew that von Braun would be able to launch the IGY satellite with Project Orbiter. But von Braun wanted to use the powerful Jupiter rocket to launch the satellite—and the Jupiter was a *missile*! The IGY satellite was to be launched in the name of peace, but the Jupiter was a weapon of war. The President felt that it wouldn't look right to use a weapon to launch a peaceful satellite.

Instead, Eisenhower turned to the Naval Research Laboratory, which had proposed its own satellite program—Project Vanguard. The Naval Laboratory planned to build a new rocket out of two older rockets called the Viking and the Aerobee, which had been used only for scientific research. Project Vanguard would be totally peaceful, as was appropriate for the launching of a scientific satellite. Project Vanguard was given the go-ahead and von Braun was turned away.

Then, in October 1957, the Soviet Union stunned the world by launching Sputnik. The "backward Russians" suddenly became the "technologically superior Russians." The United States had believed that its own technology was the most advanced in the world,

but now it wasn't so sure—and neither was the rest of the world. The Soviets had beaten the Americans into space, and the United States hadn't even realized it was in a race.

AN EMBARRASSED GIANT

The American public was angry. Congress was angry. Scientists were angry. How could such a thing be allowed to happen?

Von Braun again offered to launch a satellite using a Jupiter missile, and the White House again said no. Once again, officials turned to Project Vanguard to uphold the honor of American technology. The Naval Laboratory hastily prepared a satellite for launch on December 6, 1957.

When the launch date arrived, the attention of the nation—and of the world—was turned on a launching pad at Cape Canaveral. At 11:45 in the morning, on live television, the Vanguard rocket rose slowly into the air. It had risen about three feet when flames suddenly shot from its side. The rocket began to fall as slowly as it had risen; then it split open and exploded in a giant ball of fire.

If Vanguard couldn't rescue the United States from the embarrassment of Sputnik, perhaps von Braun could. The Army team was given permission to launch a satellite. On January 31, 1958, a modified Jupiter rocket, called Juno-1, lifted the *Explorer 1* satellite into orbit around Earth. The Soviets were no longer alone in outer space. The United States had joined them.

In the meantime the Soviets had launched another satellite into orbit, *Sputnik 2*, and this one had a living creature on board, a dog named Laika. The Soviets had proved that a living creature could survive the stresses of space flight. Less than four months after the Americans launched *Explorer 1*, the Soviets launched *Sputnik 3*, which had a complete laboratory on board.

Wernher von Braun at Cape Canaveral in 1966

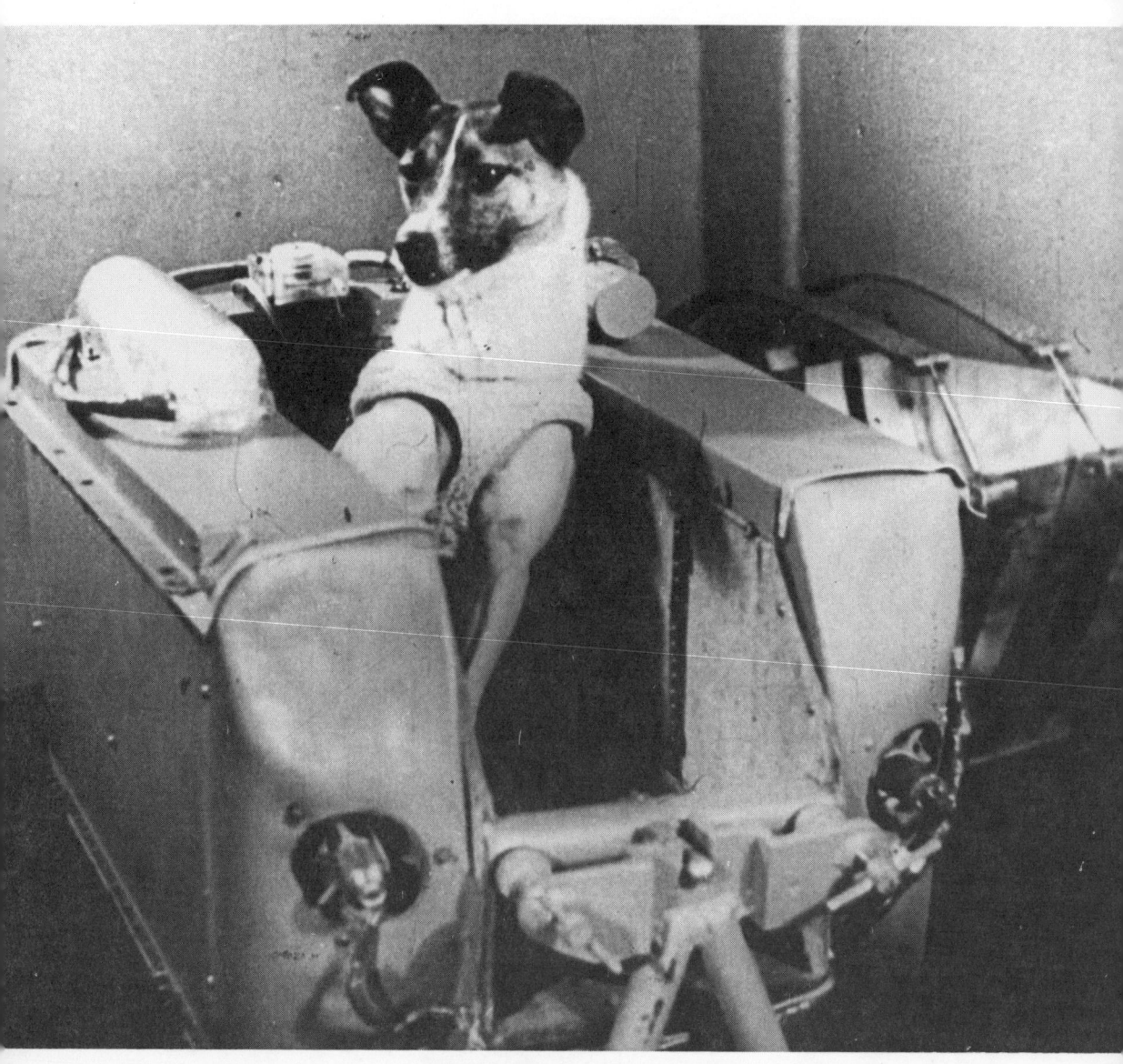

Sputnik 2's passenger, Laika

The embarrassing truth was that the Soviet satellites were big and the American satellites were very small. The ill-fated Vanguard satellite weighed 3.5 pounds (1.59 kg) and *Explorer 1* a little more than 30 pounds (13.5 kg). *Sputnik 3*, on the other hand, weighed 3,000 pounds (1,350 kg)! The reason for this was simple: the Russians had bigger, more powerful rockets.

Nevertheless, the American satellites performed important work in outer space. *Explorer 1* flew much higher than the Russian satellites and conducted experiments that led to the discovery of mysterious "belts" of radiation encircling Earth. These "belts" soon became known as the Van Allen radiation belts after the scientist James Van Allen who had designed the experiments that detected them.

But this was small consolation for Americans who felt that their country had been embarrassed by the nation they considered their greatest international rival. This was the height of the Cold War. Not only had America lost prestige in the eyes of the world, but the Soviets had shown that they could build better missiles than the United States could. Only a few months earlier, Khrushchev had felt it necessary to prove to the world that the Soviets possessed effective ICBMs. Now it was up to the United States to prove that it was the technological leader of the world—that it could build rockets every bit as good as the Soviet Union. It could build rockets that would carry large satellites—and human beings—into space.

VOYAGERS OF THE INFINITE

It was called Project Mercury, and it was the beginning of the United States manned space flight program. If it were successful, it would make the age-old dream of space travel come true. Seven men, all of them test pilots, were chosen to become the first human beings to fly in outer space.

The seven men were Alan Shepard, Virgil "Gus" Grissom, John Glenn, Malcolm Scott Carpenter, Walter Schirra, Gordon Cooper, and Donald "Deke" Slayton. From the moment their names were announced, they were heroes. Their faces appeared on television screens, the covers of magazines, the front pages of newspapers. They were as famous as movie stars, as respected as presidents.

In charge of Project Mercury was a new government agency, the National Aeronautics and Space Administration, better known as NASA. It was a civilian agency, and deliberately so. President Eisenhower wanted to show the world that the United States was exploring space in the name of peace, not in the name of the military.

The goal of Project Mercury was to send the seven astronauts, as they were known, into space one at a time in small capsules to be launched atop rockets. The first capsules would be launched on Redstone missiles. The Redstone was not the most powerful of rockets, and so these first flights would be *suborbital* flights—that is, they would not actually go into orbit, but would fly up to the edge of space and fall back into the ocean. Later spacecraft would be boosted into space atop the more powerful Atlas missile, and would actually go into orbit around Earth.

THE MERCURY CAPSULE

Although the astronauts were test pilots, they would not have a chance to do much piloting in a Mercury capsule. These were not true spaceships. The bell-shaped capsules were small and cramped, like flying sardine cans. The first model didn't even have a window; the astronaut would have to look out through a small periscope that dropped from above his head. The only control the astronaut would have over his capsule was *attitude control*—that is, he could change the way it was oriented in space, turning it sideways or backwards but not changing the direction in which it was moving.

Otherwise, the capsule was like a flying bullet, or baseball, hurled into space by the rocket, after which it would fall back to Earth like a rock. On the way back down, it would slice through the air at such a high speed that it would turn red hot from air friction. A thick heat shield on the bottom of the capsule would absorb this heat and keep the astronaut from burning up. Before it hit the ground, a parachute would open to slow the fall. Just before it smacked into the ocean, a landing bag beneath the capsule would open up, providing a cushion to ease the shock of hitting the water. The astronaut would then be "rescued" by helicopter and flown to a waiting ship.

GETTING READY TO GO

The training program for the astronauts was long and hard. Not only was it important for the astronauts to be in top physical shape, but NASA wanted to be absolutely sure that any human being, including a physically fit astronaut, could survive a trip into space.

For that reason, the astronauts were put through several years of tests.

Today, of course, we might wonder why this was necessary. Dozens of astronauts have flown in space, and most have returned unharmed. But in the late 1950s no one had ever flown in space before, and for all anyone knew it might not even be possible.

For instance, when a rocket is launched, a human being in a capsule atop that rocket is subjected to powerful acceleration forces. These are a lot like the forces that pull you back in your seat while in a rapidly accelerating car, or that pull you toward the floor in a rising elevator, but they are much, much stronger. An astronaut experiences forces many times stronger than Earth's gravity; for that reason, these forces are measured in Gs. One G is equal to the pull of Earth's gravity at Earth's surface. Experts feared that the astronauts would be disoriented by the strain of these *G forces* and would be too dizzy to monitor the many switches and gauges inside the capsule. On the way back down, the astronaut would also experience powerful G forces, as the capsule slowed down in Earth's atmosphere.

Once the spacecraft was in orbit around Earth, or coasting through the peak of a suborbital flight, all G forces would disappear, and the astronaut would be weightless. This, too, might be disorienting; human beings rarely experienced weightlessness on the surface of Earth.

To test the astronauts' response to high G forces, they were placed in a testing device called a centrifuge, in which the astronaut sat in a seat at the end of a long, rotating arm. The centrifugal force experienced in the spinning seat produced G forces similar to those the astronauts would experience during take off. It turned out that the astronauts were capable of withstanding G forces far greater than any they would experience in a Mercury capsule.

Weightlessness was simulated by sending the astronauts high aloft in the cargo bay of a jet plane, then turning off the jet engines and allowing the plane to fall back toward the ground for several minutes, as though it were a spaceship falling through suborbital flight or falling around Earth like Newton's orbiting cannonball. Just as you feel lightheaded in a rapidly plunging elevator, the astronauts floated about inside the falling jet, as weightless as they would be in outer space. Although some astronauts became sick after their first experience with weightlessness, they quickly adjusted.

As a final precaution, monkeys were sent into outer space on test flights, to see if they could perform carefully learned routines while being subjected to extreme G forces and to weightlessness. The monkeys performed well.

The rockets performed less well, and the first flight of a human astronaut was postponed again and again as scientists fine-tuned the rockets that would lift them into space, so that there would be no risk—or as little risk as possible—of losing an astronaut in flight.

ANOTHER EMBARRASSMENT

Then, on April 12, 1961, an event took place that everyone involved with the American space program had feared. The Soviets put a man in space . . . before the United States did.

The first human being in outer space was Yuri Gagarin (1934–1968). His spacecraft was called *Vostok 1*. It was launched from the Baikonur Cosmodrome (the same place the Sputnik satellites had been launched from) at a little past 9:00 in the morning, Moscow time. This was no suborbital flight. The powerful Soviet rockets lifted *Vostok 1* into orbit around Earth. During the next 108 minutes, Gagarin made a full circle of the planet; then his capsule dropped back into the atmosphere. Unlike the American Mercury capsule, which was designed to splash down in the ocean, the Soviet capsule floated down to solid ground on parachutes, though Gagarin ejected from the craft at a height of several miles and floated the rest of the way on his own parachute.

The Soviets had triumphed again, and the Americans, to put it mildly, were upset. The Mercury program had come so close to launching the first human into space, and now the Soviet Union had taken the prize!

*U.S. space monkey, Able Baker,
"reads" of his successful flight.*

*Soviet cosmonaut Yuri Gagarin is shown
here with Sergei Korolev after the
first flight of Vostok 1 in April 1961.*

THE FIRST ASTRONAUT

The first manned American spacecraft, with Alan Shepard on board, was launched from Cape Canaveral twenty-three days later, on May 5, 1961. Astronaut Shepard had nicknamed his capsule *Freedom 7*, "Freedom" for the democratic society of the United States, "7" for the seven Mercury astronauts. (The "7" also referred to the fact that Shepard's was the seventh Mercury capsule launched atop a Redstone rocket; the first six were unmanned test flights.)

Shepard lay on his back in the *Freedom 7* capsule for four hours before the launch, while engineers prepared the Redstone rocket for flight. At 9:34 Eastern Daylight Time, the rocket soared into the Florida sky, racing toward space at a top speed of 5,171 miles (8,340 km) per hour. Acceleration forces of greater than 6 Gs—six times Earth's gravity—pushed down on Shepard's body as the Redstone climbed into space.

At the top of the Redstone's flight, the *Freedom 7* capsule was released to fly unhindered through space, 116 miles (187 km) above Earth. Far below, sensitive radio monitors received information about Shepard's heartbeat and body temperature. His heartbeat was fast, but that only meant that he was excited. Otherwise, he had come through the G forces of takeoff in perfect shape. For five minutes, Shepard was weightless, floating against the straps that held him to his seat. Through his periscope, he could see a blurry view of the continents and seas far below. Briefly, Shepard was able to control the attitude (angle in relation to the horizon) of his capsule, then *Freedom 7* began the long descent back into the atmosphere.

On the trip down, air friction battered against the heat shield. Then the parachutes opened and the landing bag inflated. Fifteen minutes and twenty-two seconds after launch, Shepard's capsule splashed into the ocean. Two minutes later, a helicopter appeared above *Freedom 7* and, with Shepard's help, lifted both Shepard and the capsule out of the water and onto the deck of the aircraft carrier *Lake Champlain*.

He was only the second man in space, and had not even gone into orbit as Yuri Gagarin had, but Alan Shepard was an American hero. He received the NASA Distinguished Service Medal at the White House three days later and was given a parade in downtown Washington, D.C.

The Americans had proven once again that they had a space technology of their own, even if they were running a little behind the Russians.

Two months later, on July 21, 1961, Virgil "Gus" Grissom became the second American in space, in a Mercury capsule that he called *Liberty Bell 7*, following the naming tradition started by Alan Shepard. The flight went well until the end. After splashing into the ocean, the hatch on Grissom's capsule blew open, and Grissom was dumped accidentally into the ocean, space suit and all. As his suit filled with water, Grissom found himself pulled beneath the waves. The helicopter pilot who had come to pluck Grissom from the sea was unaware of his plight, and tried to lift the capsule first. But the capsule had filled with water and was too heavy to lift; finally, the pilot let it fall back into the sea, where it was never recovered. He then lifted Grissom, who he now realized was on the verge of drowning, from the ocean. Shaken, Grissom was flown to the deck of the aircraft carrier *Randolph*.

THE SECOND COSMONAUT

On August 6, 1961, word reached the United States that the Soviets had launched a second man, Gherman Titov, into orbit around Earth. Titov remained in space for more than twenty-five hours, becoming the first astronaut—or cosmonaut, as the Soviets called them—to sleep while in orbit. He complained later that his weightless hands drifted aimlessly in the cabin while he tried to sleep; finally, he was forced to slip them under his seatbelt to hold them down. His worst problem, though, was space sickness. From the moment he became weightless, Titov was nauseous. He fought it off, though, and recovered before his mission had to be aborted. Although Titov was the first person to suffer from space sickness, he was not the last.

JOHN GLENN AND
FRIENDSHIP 7

Originally, NASA had planned to send every astronaut in the Mercury program on a suborbital flight before any astronauts were sent on orbital flights. But the flights of Shepard and Grissom had shown that astronauts could handle spaceflight, and the Soviets were getting too far ahead of the Americans to allow Project Mercury to dawdle. So it was agreed that the next flight would put an astronaut in orbit atop an Atlas rocket.

The astronaut chosen for that flight was John Glenn, who soared into space in his capsule *Friendship 7*. At 9:47 on the morning of February 20, 1962, Glenn rose 162 miles (261 km) above Earth, circling the planet three times in five hours.

Each time around Earth, Glenn noticed a peculiar phenomenon outside his capsule window that has been reported by other astronauts as well, but never fully explained. Strange, glowing "fireflies" appeared alongside his craft, following him in orbit for several minutes. These became known as "John Glenn's fireflies" and may have been caused by ice particles shedding from the capsule's hull.

About halfway through the flight, NASA's ground controllers (including Alan Shepard, who was in charge of communicating with the capsule) became aware that something was wrong. An indicator on a control panel showed that Glenn's landing bag had popped into place, ready for splashdown. But the landing bag wasn't supposed to open until the parachutes had opened on the way back down. If it had opened prematurely, then the heat shield wouldn't work properly . . . and Glenn would burn up as he fell through the atmosphere.

The ground controllers were unsure if the landing bag had really opened or if they were receiving a false signal. They suspected it was a false signal, but they couldn't take that chance. They told Glenn to leave his retro-rockets, which were used for attitude control, in place during his return to Earth, so that they could absorb the heat of the air friction. (Normally, they would have been dropped from the capsule before reentry.)

On the way back to Earth, Glenn saw burning pieces of hull flash past his window, and feared for a moment that his heat shield was disintegrating! If this had happened, Glenn would have died during the descent; but the burning pieces must have come from his retro-rocket pack instead.

If Alan Shepard had been a hero after his spaceflight, Glenn became a superhero. He was given parades in both Washington, D.C., and New York, addressed a packed house at the United Nations, and was mobbed by admirers in his hometown. Some years later, he entered politics, and became a United States senator from Ohio.

FLIGHTS THAT FOLLOWED

There were three more Mercury orbital flights after Glenn; Donald Slayton was removed from the program because of a suspected heart problem, though he finally flew in space years later as part of the Apollo–Soyuz project (see chapter seven).

Scott Carpenter orbited Earth three times in his capsule, *Aurora 7*, on May 24, 1962. His mission ran into an unusual problem: too many scientific experiments. Because every experiment he had been asked to perform required that he change the attitude of his capsule, he quickly ran out of the fuel necessary to control the craft, and so had barely enough to break out of orbit and return to Earth. And, due to bad timing, his capsule splashed down about 250 miles (403 km) from its intended landing place.

The fact that Carpenter had run out of fuel worried engineers on the ground, who had planned to include at least one longer mission in Project Mercury but now feared that the capsule had too little fuel capacity to allow the astronaut to stay in space for more than three orbits. On the next mission, astronaut Walter Schirra demonstrated that, in fact, it was possible to perform a six-orbit mission and still have plenty of fuel in reserve when the craft returned to Earth. Schirra flew his six orbits in the capsule *Sigma 7* on October 3, 1962.

John Glenn is given a hero's welcome on completion of his Friendship 7 space flight. To Glenn's right is President John Kennedy.

Schirra's fuel conservation opened the way for Gordon Cooper's mission in *Faith 7* on May 15, 1963. Cooper orbited Earth twenty-two-and-a-half times in thirty-four hours, becoming the first American to remain in space for more than a day. This gave Cooper a lot of time to observe the ground below, and he reported at great length on what he saw. Scientists on Earth were surprised to learn that Cooper could see houses, highways, and automobiles, which no one had believed would be visible from such a height.

The *Faith 7* mission ended the Mercury program, but the Soviets were not asleep while the Americans were sending astronauts orbiting Earth. In August 1962, the Soviets startled the world by sending two space capsules into orbit at the same time, launching the capsules only a day apart. The capsules passed within a few miles of one another. Scientists in the United States wondered if the Russians were developing techniques for rendezvousing capsules in space—that is, bringing two capsules together so that their occupants could share capsules and equipment.

In June 1963, shortly after the end of the Mercury program, the Russians launched two more cosmonauts into space in separate capsules. One of them was Valentina Tereshkova, the first woman in space.

When Project Mercury began, no one knew what would follow it. By the time of John Glenn's flight, however, bold plans had been made for America's future in space. The most spectacular—and expensive—scientific project in human history had been set in motion.

The president of the United States announced that Americans were on their way . . . to the moon!

CHAPTER

ONE SMALL STEP
FOR A MAN . . .

By the early 1960s, it was no secret that the Soviet Union and the United States were engaged in a space race. And by 1963, the Russians were a couple of laps ahead. They had placed the first satellite in orbit and the first human in space. They had won a few minor prizes as well: larger satellites, longer space trips for their astronauts, two capsules in orbit at one time.

The idea of a space race between the two most powerful nations on Earth might seem a little silly today, but during the Cold War it was taken very seriously. The Soviet Union wasn't really showing the United States that it could build better spaceships. It was saying, in a secret code that almost everybody could read, that the Soviet way of life was better than the American way of life. And, more important, it was demonstrating that it could build better missiles and deliver bigger bombs.

When Yuri Gagarin became the first human being in space, American prestige suffered. The newly elected United States president, John F. Kennedy, knew that he had to do something to win back that lost prestige—and, not incidentally, to boost his own popularity, which suffered along with the nation's prestige.

Kennedy knew that only a truly spectacular achievement in outer space would impress the Soviets—and the rest of the world—with American technological ingenuity. What could be more spectacular than sending Americans all the way to the moon?

"BEFORE THIS DECADE IS OUT . . ."

On May 25, 1961, a little more than a month after Gagarin's orbit and twenty days after Alan Shepard's brief visit to the edge of space, Kennedy spoke these famous words to Congress,

> *I believe this nation should commit itself to achieving the goal, before this decade is out, of landing a man on the moon and returning him safely to Earth. No single space project in this period will be so impressive to mankind, or more important for the long-range exploration of space, and none will be more difficult or expensive to accomplish.*

With those words, Kennedy set in motion the machinery for sending an American to the moon. The most impressive words in his speech, though, were "before this decade is out." That gave NASA eight-and-one-half years to reach the moon, at a time when no American had yet orbited Earth! Sadly, Kennedy did not live to see if his lunar deadline was met. He was assassinated on November 22, 1963. In his honor, the name of the NASA launching center at Cape Canaveral, Florida, was changed to Cape Kennedy, though years later it came to be known as Cape Canaveral once again.

PROJECT GEMINI

The first part of the lunar program was named Project Gemini, after a mythical pair of Greek twins, because the new space capsule would seat two astronauts instead of one. Indeed, the new Gemini capsule was far more spacious than the cramped Mercury craft, and was much closer to a true spaceship: not only could the astronauts control the attitude of the capsule, they could actually "fly" it, moving it into new orbits if they so desired. The Gemini capsule would be fired into space by the new, more powerful Titan II rocket, a modified version of the Air Force Titan.

The aim of the Gemini program—one of the aims, at least— was to train astronauts to be true space pilots. No longer would astronauts sit helplessly in a capsule that sped through space like a bullet; now they would learn to guide their spaceship through space, using skills that would be important when it was time to go to the moon. Eleven new astronauts had been recruited for the program, and several of the Mercury astronauts also joined up.

Before the first Gemini flight could be launched, though, the Soviets startled the world with two more firsts. On October 12, 1964, *Voskhod 1* carried three cosmonauts into space in a single, rather crowded capsule. And on March 18, 1965, two more cosmonauts orbited earth in *Voskhod 2*. One of them, Alexei Leonov, became the first person to step outside of his space capsule and float in space protected only by his space suit. This was the first *spacewalk*, or *EVA (extravehicular activity)*.

Undaunted, the Americans launched *Gemini 3*—the first manned Gemini flight—on March 23, 1965. The crewmen were Virgil Grissom, now a veteran astronaut, and rookie John Young. After the flight, Young was chastised for having smuggled aboard a corned beef sandwich, against NASA regulations.

Two new astronauts, James McDivitt and Edward White, spent four days in space after being launched on June 3, 1965, in *Gemini 4*. During the flight, White became the first American to walk in space, guiding himself about with a gas thruster that he held in his arms. In effect, White became the first human spaceship (though he was tethered to the main spacecraft by a long cable).

In *Gemini 5*, astronauts Gordon Cooper and Pete Conrad set a new endurance record by spending eight days in orbit, but the record was broken four months later when *Gemini 7* astronauts Frank Borman and James Lovell spent fourteen days in space. *Gemini 7*, which was launched in December 1965, was joined shortly after by *Gemini 6*, crewed by astronauts Walter Schirra and Thomas

*In June 1965, astronaut Edward White,
tethered to Gemini 4, walks in space.*

Stafford. The two space teams maneuvered their capsules within 6 feet (2 m) of one another, closer together than any Soviet capsules had ever come, demonstrating the ability of American astronauts to maneuver skillfully in space.

The next flight, *Gemini 8*, almost ended in tragedy. Shortly before the manned launch, NASA used an Atlas rocket to lift a smaller Agena rocket into orbit around Earth. Astronauts Neil Armstrong and David Scott then attempted to dock their Gemini capsule with the Agena—that is, to actually insert one end of the capsule inside the Agena rocket, as if they were assembling a larger spacecraft in outer space.

They succeeded, but after the docking the Gemini capsule began to twist and turn uncontrollably. The astronauts undocked from the Agena, but the twisting and turning continued. If the astronauts had been unable to control their spacecraft, they might have become marooned in space, doomed to orbit Earth until their oxygen supply ran out. Fortunately, they were finally able to bring it under control, and made an early return to Earth, landing at an emergency site on the opposite side of the world from their planned splashdown site.

After four more flights, which introduced astronauts Eugene Cernan, Michael Collins, Richard F. Gordon, and Edwin Aldrin to orbital flight, Project Gemini ended in December 1966. Not only was it a success, not only had it trained a group of astronauts in the skills needed to fly a true spaceship, but it had put the United States ahead of schedule in its plans to voyage to the moon. It looked as if the first lunar flight might come as soon as 1967.

But the United States had been lucky during its first five years of sending humans into space. Despite harrowingly close calls such as the one experienced by Armstrong and Scott, no astronaut had yet died in the line of duty. This run of luck was about to end.

PROJECT APOLLO

When NASA officials had first seriously studied the possibility of sending astronauts to the moon, they had decided to build a new rocket that would be equal to the task. This superrocket was to be called Nova. It would fly to the moon, land on the surface, and fly back to Earth. It was to be the most powerful rocket ever built.

Alas, Nova was never to be. It was too expensive, would take too long to build, and, NASA believed, wasn't really necessary.

Instead, it was decided that the moon ship should be a *modular* craft—that is, it would be built of three independent units, each of which would play a role in the mission. These units were the Command Module (or CM), the Service Module (or SM), and the Lunar Module (or LM). (See illustrations on the facing page of Command Module and Service Module.) Assembled, these three modules would make a complete spaceship, capable of going to the moon and back. However, the entire spaceship was designed to take off from Earth orbit rather than from Earth itself. So a rocket would be needed to get the lunar craft into orbit around Earth. For this job, Wernher von Braun and his team of rocket engineers set to work designing a new rocket called the Saturn. While not as powerful as the Nova would have been, Saturn would still be the most powerful rocket on Earth.

Here's how the three parts of the lunar spaceship would be used during the flight:

The Command Module would be a larger version of the capsules in which astronauts had orbited Earth in Projects Mercury and Gemini. It was where the astronauts would live during the trip to and from the moon.

The Service Module would contain the life-support systems for the Command Module. It would also hold the rocket that would bring the astronauts back from the moon.

The Lunar Module would be a tiny spacecraft in its own right. While the Command Module orbited around the moon, the Lunar Module would take two astronauts to the lunar surface . . . and back to the Command Module. A third astronaut would remain in the Command Module while the other two explored the lunar surface.

The moon program was dubbed Project Apollo, after the Greek god who pulled the sun across the sky with his chariot. The first

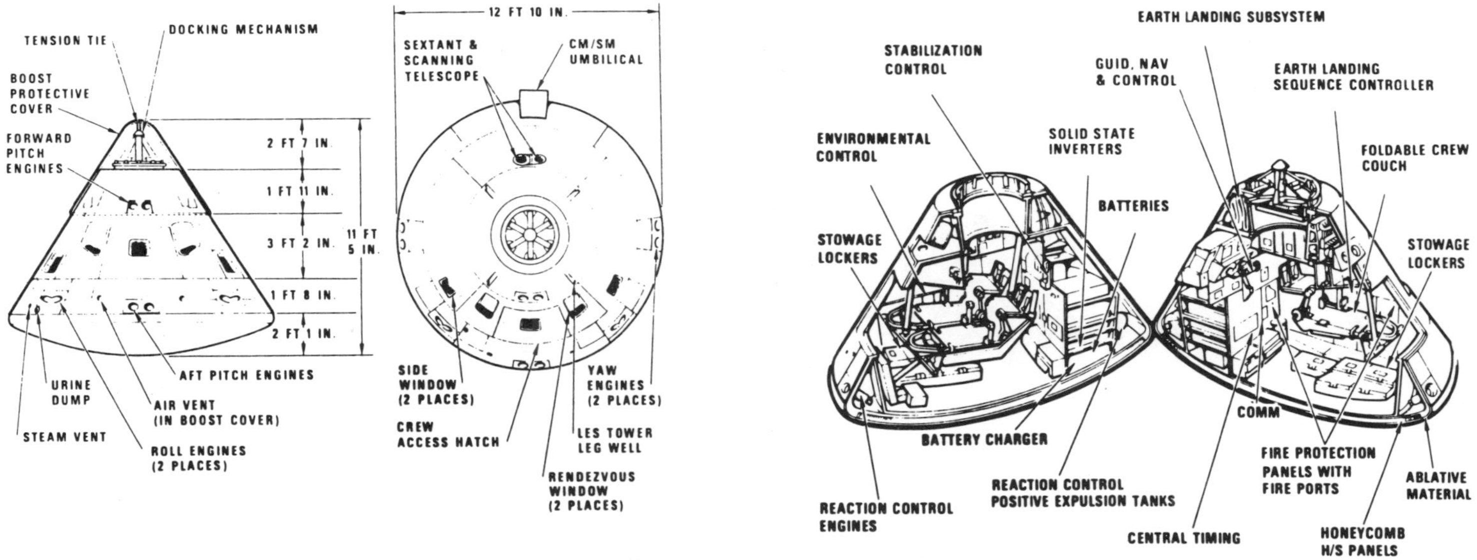

COMMAND MODULE

EARTH LANDING SUBSYSTEM

STABILIZATION CONTROL

GUID. NAV & CONTROL

SOLID STATE INVERTERS

BATTERIES

ENVIRONMENTAL CONTROL

STOWAGE LOCKERS

REACTION CONTROL ENGINES

BATTERY CHARGER

REACTION CONTROL POSITIVE EXPULSION TANKS

CENTRAL TIMING

COMM

FIRE PROTECTION PANELS WITH FIRE PORTS

HONEYCOMB N/S PANELS

ABLATIVE MATERIAL

FOLDABLE CREW COUCH

STOWAGE LOCKERS

EARTH LANDING SEQUENCE CONTROLLER

12 FT 10 IN.

CM/SM UMBILICAL

SEXTANT & SCANNING TELESCOPE

YAW ENGINES (2 PLACES)

LES TOWER LEG WELL

RENDEZVOUS WINDOW (2 PLACES)

SIDE WINDOW (2 PLACES)

CREW ACCESS HATCH

DOCKING MECHANISM

TENSION TIE

BOOST PROTECTIVE COVER

FORWARD PITCH ENGINES

AIR VENT (IN BOOST COVER)

AFT PITCH ENGINES

ROLL ENGINES (2 PLACES)

URINE DUMP

STEAM VENT

2 FT 7 IN.

1 FT 11 IN.

11 FT 5 IN.

3 FT 2 IN.

1 FT 8 IN.

2 FT 1 IN.

SERVICE MODULE

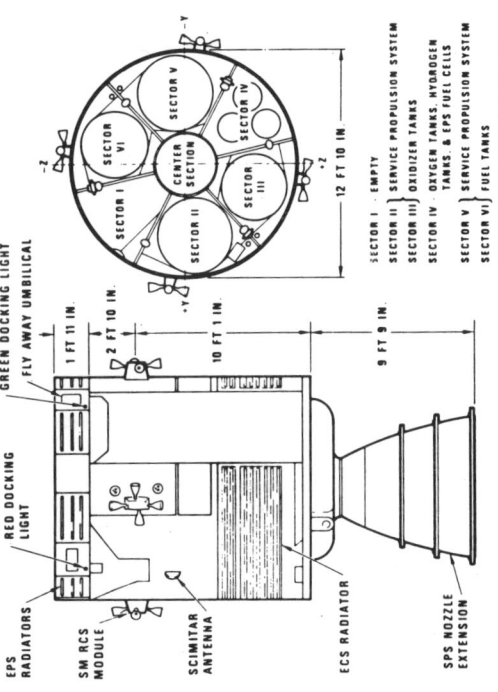

SECTION I   EMPTY

SECTION II   SERVICE PROPULSION SYSTEM

SECTION III OXIDIZER TANKS

SECTION IV   OXYGEN TANKS, HYDROGEN TANKS & EPS FUEL CELLS

SECTION V   SERVICE PROPULSION SYSTEM

SECTION VI   FUEL TANKS

CENTER SECTION   SERVICE PROPULSION SYSTEM HELIUM TANKS

12 FT 10 IN.

SECTION VI

SECTION V

SECTION IV

CENTER SECTION

SECTION I

SECTION II

SECTION III

GREEN DOCKING LIGHT

FLY AWAY UMBILICAL

RED DOCKING LIGHT

EPS RADIATORS

SM RCS MODULE

SCIMITAR ANTENNA

ECS RADIATOR

SPS NOZZLE EXTENSION

1 FT 11 IN.

2 FT 10 IN.

10 FT 7 IN.

9 FT 9 IN.

Apollo flight was scheduled for early 1967. It would not go to the moon, but would test the lunar spaceship in Earth orbit. The astronauts on board were to be Virgil Grissom (the second man in space), Edward White (the first American to walk in space), and Roger Chaffee (a rookie who had never been in space before).

On January 27, 1967, the three astronauts arrived at the launching pad for a routine test of their spacecraft, which was not to be launched for at least two or three more weeks. Donning their spacesuits, the astronauts entered the craft and sat in the couches that they would occupy during the flight. The hatch was sealed behind them. The equipment tests began.

At exactly 6:31 in the evening, something went wrong. A small electric power surge was picked up by sensors outside the spacecraft. Seconds later, astronaut Grissom's voice crackled over the intercom: "Fire! We've got a fire in the cockpit!" His voice was horrified, as well it should have been. The atmosphere inside the spacecraft was pure oxygen, and fires burn very quickly in pure oxygen. There was no time to get the astronauts out!

White tried to unbolt the door, but he wasn't fast enough, and the door wasn't designed to be opened in a hurry. Within seconds, flames could be seen licking at the inside of the Command Module. A voice that might have been Roger Chaffee's screamed from inside: "We've got a bad fire—let's get out . . . We're burning up!" It was the last thing any of the astronauts had a chance to say. The fire rushed through the capsule, splitting open the hull. By the time rescuers were able to force their way into the burnt Command Module, the astronauts were dead.

The astronauts were given military funerals at Arlington National Cemetery and at West Point (for White). The Apollo program was put on hold while NASA officials investigated the cause of the tragic accident.

Three months later, the Russians also experienced a tragedy in space. The parachute that was intended to bring a new spacecraft, *Soyuz 1*, back from space became entangled as the capsule dropped through the atmosphere. The capsule's occupant, cosmonaut Vladimir Komarov, was killed instantly when the spacecraft smashed into the ground. The Soviet space program also came to a halt. Between April 1967 and October 1968, there were no manned space missions launched anywhere in the world.

"IN THE BEGINNING . . ."

The Apollo spacecraft was redesigned so that another terrible accident like the one that took the lives of Grissom, White, and Chaffee would not occur . . . or so the craft's designers hoped. After a year and a half of delays, the first Apollo mission—*Apollo 7*—was launched on October 11, 1968. On board were Walter Schirra, Donn Eisele, and Walter Cunningham. The spacecraft orbited Earth for eleven days, and the equipment passed all tests with flying colors. The craft was boosted into orbit by a Saturn IB rocket, a smaller version of the Saturn V rocket that was to carry the spacecraft to the moon.

Although the next Apollo flight was not originally intended to go to the moon, NASA was now beginning to worry that the Soviets were planning a moon flight of their own—and might get there first if Project Apollo did not proceed with all due speed. The idea of letting the Soviets steal yet another space first away from the Americans was unthinkable. *Apollo 8* was given the go-ahead to orbit once around the moon and return to Earth.

Astronauts Frank Borman, James Lovell, and William Anders lifted off from Cape Canaveral on December 21, 1968, atop a Saturn V rocket. It was not the first time a Saturn V had been used to launch human beings into space, but it was the first time a Saturn V—the biggest rocket ever built—had been used in an orbital mission of any kind. It worked flawlessly. The Apollo spacecraft went into orbit around Earth, and the final decision was made to send the craft to the moon.

The trip to the moon took three days. On Christmas Eve the Apollo spacecraft went into orbit around the moon, circling it ten times. Television pictures of the moon's surface were sent back to Earth. On Christmas Day, the astronauts read aloud the opening passages of the book of Genesis to the television audience nearly 240,000 miles (386,400 km) away on Earth.

Finally, the rocket in the Service Module was fired and the spacecraft left lunar orbit and returned to Earth. Only the Command Module splashed down in the ocean upon the craft's return, the Service Module having been released as planned upon reentering Earth's atmosphere. The trip had lasted six days.

Apollo 9 did not go to the moon. It remained in Earth orbit, where astronauts McDivitt, Scott, and Schweickart tested the Lunar Module. Apollo 10 circled the moon as Apollo 8 had, but this time two astronauts, Stafford and Cernan, flew the lunar module low over the surface of the moon, while astronaut John Young waited in the orbiting Command Module. The lunar module flew within 10 miles (16 km) of the moon's surface, then returned to the Command Module as planned.

ONE GIANT LEAP FOR MANKIND

The flight for which everyone was waiting, Apollo 11, left Cape Kennedy at 7:00 in the morning on July 16, 1969. Three days later, on July 19, astronauts Neil Armstrong, Edwin Aldrin, and Michael Collins went into orbit around the moon. On the historic morning of July 20, Armstrong and Aldrin entered the Lunar Module, which they had nicknamed "Eagle," and descended to the moon. When they touched down on the surface, in the lunar region known as the Sea of Tranquility, Armstrong radioed to NASA's Mission Control Center in Houston, Texas: "Houston, Tranquility Base here. The Eagle has landed."

Kennedy's dream had become a reality—and it had happened, as promised, before the end of the decade. Americans had landed on the moon!

When Armstrong descended the ladder from the Lunar Module to the moon's surface, he spoke the historic words: "That's one small step for a man, one giant leap for mankind." This "small step" was broadcast live on television all over the planet Earth, via a TV camera on one of the legs of the Lunar Module.

*Astronauts Neil Armstrong and Edwin Aldrin place
the U.S. flag on the surface of the moon on July 20, 1969.*

Armstrong and Aldrin gathered moon rocks, planted an American flag in the lunar soil, and talked by radio to United States President Richard Nixon. They took off in their Lunar Module on July 21, returning to the Command Module, nicknamed Columbia, where fellow astronaut Collins was waiting for them.

The astronauts returned to Earth on July 24. The first manned lunar landing was history.

CHAPTER

7

FROM SKYLAB
TO THE SHUTTLE

What do you do after you've gone to the moon?

For NASA, the answer was simple. You go to Mars.

In 1969, a special Presidential Space Task Group pondered the question of what the United States should do next in space. Their answer was that a manned mission should be launched toward the planet Mars sometime in the 1980s. Preparations should begin immediately.

This recommendation was given to President Richard Nixon. The president liked the idea, but was cautious. A Mars project would be very expensive, and the space program simply wasn't as popular as it had been in the early 1960s.

Project Apollo had been proposed during the Cold War, when the American public was genuinely frightened that the Soviet Union would land on the moon before the United States did. But by 1969 the Cold War was over, and the United States had soundly beaten the Soviets to the moon. The public had lost interest in spending large amounts of money to send astronauts to the moon, or anywhere else.

Not only was money not available for a mission to Mars, but it also wasn't available to send as many Apollo flights to the moon as NASA had originally planned. Several missions were canceled over the protests of scientists. NASA was forced to scale back its plans for future missions into space.

THE LAST APOLLOS

The remaining moon missions went well, though, with one exception. As the unlucky *Apollo 13* spacecraft rocketed toward the moon on April 13, 1970 (which was not, as it happens, a Friday), an oxygen tank blew up in the Service Module. Astronauts Lovell, Haise, and Swigert found themselves with almost no oxygen and little power. In desperation, the crew moved into the Lunar Module, nicknamed "Aquarius," still attached to the other two modules, to use its oxygen and power supply. Unfortunately, there was no way to turn the craft around and head back to Earth, so the three astronauts were forced to spend four days huddled together in the Lunar Module, as it circled the moon and sailed back to Earth.

The last lunar flight, *Apollo 17*, ended on December 7, 1972. It was the end of an era, the last visit to the Moon by a human being of any nationality (at least as of 1987).

In 1973, however, NASA used leftover Apollo equipment to realize an old dream of Tsiolkovsky's: a space station in orbit around Earth, where human beings could live for long periods of time. The Skylab space station was a giant cylinder in space, larger than any spacecraft ever put into orbit, with winglike solar panels to supply it with power and living space inside for three astronauts. Between May 1973, and February 1974, three crews of astronauts visited the space station, docking with it in an Apollo spacecraft fitted out for orbital flight. The last crew stayed for eighty-four days, the longest anyone had stayed in space up until that time. They proved, if the proof should ever be needed, that human beings might be able to remain in space for long voyages, such as would be needed to reach Mars, or for extended duty in a permanent space station.

The last Apollo flight did not go to the moon. In 1975, the so-called Apollo-Soyuz test project mission united American and Soviet spacemen for the first (and last) time in a joint space venture. For two days, three American astronauts and two Soviet cosmonauts orbited Earth together in their docked spacecraft, performing scientific experiments and swapping jokes. The Americans were Thomas Stafford, Vance Brand, and Donald Slayton (the only one of the Mercury astronauts denied the chance to fly in a Mercury capsule). The Soviets were Alexei Lenov, the first man to walk in space, and Valery Kubasov.

It was the last time that Americans would venture into space for six years. The next time, they would be flying a spacecraft unlike anything that had been flown before.

THE SPACE SHUTTLE

Rockets are expensive. They are difficult to build, cost a lot of money, and are usually thrown away after one use. Throwing away a Saturn V rocket after one mission to the moon has been compared to building an ocean liner, sailing it once across the ocean, and then sinking it.

NASA had known all along that the future of space travel was in reusable spacecraft, not disposable rockets. The spaceship of the future would be used again and again. It would be expensive to build, but cheap to reuse.

What NASA needed was a space shuttle.

Permission was granted in 1972 to build such a craft. Several plans were drawn up, then discarded. Finally, it was decided that the shuttle would be a hybrid of rocket and airplane, made up of three very different parts.

The most important part was the Orbiter. Looking much like a big, sleek passenger airplane, the Orbiter would be a true spacecraft, designed to orbit Earth, then glide to a soft landing. But the Orbiter would be launched like a rocket, and for this reason it would need a large fuel tank, and two extra booster rockets. These boosters, called the solid rocket boosters (or SRBs) would be strapped to both sides of the shuttle before launch. They were solid-fuel rockets that would be dropped from the shuttle as soon as they had burnt up all their fuel. Later, they would be retrieved from the ocean and reused. The tank would supply fuel to the main rocket engines built into the shuttle itself. Once the shuttle was up to speed, this tank would be dropped as well, though it would not be recovered.

NASA envisioned a fleet of four shuttles that would be able to perform space missions on an almost weekly basis. They would completely replace disposable rockets. All civilian satellites, and many military ones, would be launched by the shuttle, and scientific experiments would be performed on it as well.

This isn't quite how it worked out, though NASA came very close to achieving this dream.

After years of delay, the first orbital flight of a space shuttle came on April 12, 1981, the twentieth anniversary of Yuri Gagarin's historic flight. Astronauts John Young and Robert Crippen flew the shuttle *Columbia* on a two-day orbital test mission. On April 14, after a successful mission, they landed the craft on the runway at Edward's Air Force Base in California, the first time any spacecraft had ever taxied to a soft landing after flying in outer space.

Over the next four years, three more shuttles joined the fleet: *Challenger*, *Discovery*, and *Atlantis*. The shuttle flights chalked up many firsts in outer space. In November 1983, the shuttle *Columbia* carried a full scientific laboratory called Spacelab, built by the European Space Agency (ESA), into orbit. In April 1984, astronauts performed the first repair of a satellite in orbit. The first American woman astronaut, Sally Ride, rode the shuttle in June 1983. The first black American astronaut, Guion Bluford, soared aloft on the shuttle in August 1983.

But in 1986 tragedy struck the shuttle—and the United States space program came to a sudden halt.

On the morning of January 28, the crew of shuttle flight 51-L boarded the space shuttle *Challenger*. There were seven in the crew: Francis Scobee, Michael Smith, Judith Resnick, Ronald McNair, Ellison Onizuka, Gregory Jarvis, and Christa McAuliffe. McAuliffe was a high school teacher who had been chosen to fly in space as part of a newly inaugurated "Citizen in Space" program.

The historic photograph of the explosion of the space shuttle Challenger shortly after takeoff on January 28, 1986.

At 11:38 A.M., *Challenger* lifted off from the launchpad at Cape Canaveral. Less than two minutes later, in a terrible explosion that has since been seen again and again on videotape around the world, it was gone. No crew members survived. The debris of the orbiter, the fuel tank, and the boosters fell slowly into the Atlantic Ocean 9 miles (15 km) below.

What destroyed the space shuttle *Challenger*? Extensive investigation after the accident showed that it was almost certainly due to a faulty device called an O-ring, which held the sections of the solid rocket boosters together. Investigators believed that an O-ring slipped and allowed hot flames from the booster to touch the external tank. The explosion followed almost instantly.

But the investigation also showed that the concern for safety that had marked NASA's years of sending astronauts into orbit and to the moon in the 1960s and early 1970s may have slipped as well. Officials at NASA, under pressure to fly an increasing number of missions in 1986, had known that the O-rings might be faulty and had allowed the *Challenger* to fly anyway.

Seven astronauts paid for that mistake with their lives.

CHAPTER

A FUTURE
IN SPACE?

Rockets have taken us into space, around the world, and to the moon. And while astronauts were using rockets to open new horizons for human beings in space, other rockets were carrying automated probes to almost all of the planets of the solar system—Mercury, Venus, Mars, Jupiter, Saturn, and Uranus—to radio back information and photographs of places that human beings may not explore in our lifetimes. Thousands of satellites orbit overhead, relaying television pictures around the world, or taking pictures of cloud formations far below to help meteorologists predict the weather, or photographing entire continents so that geologists can study the nature of mountains and ecologists can study forests and deserts and cartographers can make maps, or taking secret pictures of military installations for the eyes of military commanders.

Rockets have brought us many wonders. They have carried astronauts to the moon, but they have also given us live television broadcasts from Tokyo and five-day weather forecasts and maps of unsurpassed accuracy, and the ability to spy on other countries from afar.

But what of the future? Will rockets take us farther into space?

Will human beings travel to Mars, Venus . . . and to planets orbiting distant stars?

Probably they will.

The space program will go on. In the twenty-first century, we may go to Mars and beyond. A trip across such vast distances will take a long time, and new rockets and spacecraft will need to be designed to meet the challenge.

The stars will be a special challenge. As we saw in chapter two, even the nearest stars are trillions of miles distant, so far away that light takes several years to travel from those stars to Earth.

The great physicist Albert Einstein showed us long ago that it is not possible to travel faster than the speed of light. If a star is four light years away—that is, the distance that light travels in four years—we cannot hope to make the trip in less than four years, and there is little chance that a rocket could be built that would travel even that fast. More likely, the trip would take thousands of years. Generations of astronauts would live out their lives during such a trip. Star travel is not for the impatient.

Echoing the works of Konstantin Tsiolkovsky, Princeton University professor Gerard O'Neill has suggested that we build giant cylinders in space that he calls space colonies, in which thousands of people could live amid Earthlike surroundings while orbiting partway between the Earth and the moon. Perhaps someday such a space colony will choose to leave the Earth–moon system and rocket away into space, becoming the first starship.

But there is another side to rocketry, a dark side, and it will also have an effect on our future.

Most of the rockets in the world today are intercontinental ballistic missiles, intended to carry deadly nuclear weapons in the event of a worldwide war. The United States has thousands of these ICBMs, buried in silos beneath the ground or carried aboard submarines, mostly aimed at the Soviet Union. And the Soviet Union also has thousands of ICBMs, mostly aimed at the United States.

An ICBM would take roughly thirty minutes to fly from the United States to the Soviet Union or vice versa. It would spend only a few minutes rising through the atmosphere, dropping its multiple stages as it climbed. Then the bus (the platform atop the rocket that contains the nuclear warheads) would coast through space in suborbital flight, just as Alan Shepard had coasted through space in his *Freedom 7* capsule. Once it was above the enemy country, it would release its warheads at targets far below. Each warhead would explode in a huge nuclear explosion.

This is the irony of rocketry. All of the great rocket pioneers—Tsiolkovsky, Goddard, von Braun, Korolev—believed that rockets should be used to carry humans into space. And yet all except Tsiolkovsky worked at one time or another building missiles intended as weapons . . . because it was the only way that they could interest their governments in building rockets.

If nuclear war happens, it will very likely be the end of the world as we know it. No one wins a nuclear war. The explosions may alter the climate of Earth so severely that a nuclear winter will settle over the world.

There are scientists who believe that we can use rockets to fight rockets, satellites to fight missiles. In 1983, President Ronald Reagan inaugurated a program called the Strategic Defense Initiative that will build satellites that will use lasers and other futuristic weapons to shoot down ICBMs. If this program, nicknamed Star Wars, is successful, it will put an end to the threat posed by the rockets we call ICBMs.

But there are other scientists who believe that the Star Wars counterweapons won't work, and that they might make nuclear war more likely.

Who's right? No one knows yet. The technology of rockets, given to us by scientists like Tsiolkovsky, Goddard, von Braun, and Korolev, can still be used to make war or to make peace. But the best use of all will be to carry us to the other planets—and, eventually, to the stars.

GLOSSARY

Atoms—the tiny particles that make up all matter, including the gas that is ejected from a rocket.

Attitude control—the ability to change the orientation of a space capsule, but not the direction in which it is traveling.

Escape velocity—the speed at which a rocket must be traveling in order to escape from Earth's gravity.

EVA (extravehicular activity)—anything that an astronaut does outside of his or her spacecraft.

G forces—the gravitylike forces created by the acceleration of a spacecraft.

Intercontinental ballistic missiles (ICBMs)—rockets used to carry bombs across long distances.

Launch vehicle—the rocket that propels a spacecraft from the surface of Earth into outer space.

Liquid-fuel rocket—a rocket that burns a liquid rather than a solid fuel.

Molecules—chains of atoms.

Orbital velocity—the speed at which a rocket must be traveling in order to boost a spacecraft into orbit around Earth.

Outer space—everything beyond Earth's atmosphere.

Satellite—an object orbiting around another object, such as the moon around Earth.

Solar System—the sun and all of its satellites, including Earth and the eight other planets.

Solid-fuel rocket—a rocket that burns a solid rather than a liquid fuel.

Spacewalk—a trip by an astronaut outside of his or her spacecraft (usually while tethered to the spacecraft).

Sputnik—the first artificial Earth satellite, launched by the Soviet Union in 1957.

Suborbital flight—a flight into outer space that does not go into orbit around Earth but instead falls back to the ground.

FOR FURTHER
READING

Baker, David. *The History of Manned Space Flight.* New York: Crown, 1985.

_____. *The Rocket.* New York: Crown, 1978.

Although not particularly easy to read, these exhaustive books contain just about everything you might need to know about the history of rockets and space travel.

Lewis, Richard S. *Appointment on the Moon.* New York: Viking, 1969.

A readable history of the development of space travel up through the Apollo moon landing, by a reporter who was present for many of the events he writes about.

Ley, Willy. *Rockets, Missiles, and Men in Space.* New York: Viking, 1968.

A classic, entertaining history of rocketry and space travel up through the beginning of project Apollo, by one of the foremost historians in the field.

Nicolson, Iain. *Sputnik to Space Shuttle.* New York: Dodd, Mead, 1985.

Compact and readable history of space flight by a professor of astronomy and veteran science writer.

Von Braun, Wernher. *Space Frontier.* New York: Holt, Rinehart & Winston, 1971.

Clearly written essays on rocketry and space travel, by the man who supervised the building of the German V-2 rocket and the Saturn 5 rocket that launched Apollo toward the moon.

Von Braun, Wernher, and Ordway, Frederick. *History of Rocketry and Space Travel.* New York: Crowell, 1969.
——. *Space Travel.* New York: Harper & Row, 1985.

Two editions of a definitive history of space travel by a rocket expert and a rocketry historian.

INDEX